Introduction

You may think that using thick yarns and big needles means that your knitted creations will not be as valuable as items using finer yarns and taking 10 times the hourly commitment. But you'll find these outstanding designs make it clear that you don't have to invest weeks or months on a fashionable wearable or special gift knit.

The Stripe-It-Rich Turtleneck and Stylish Bolero are great to make for yourself or for friends and family. From a cuddly baby blanket to hat, muff and scarf set and cuffed cap, you'll enjoy the fast progress you'll make when using larger needles.

All of our projects are created with worsted or bulky yarns on size 10½, 11 and 13 needles, which you may not have used before. If this is so, please see our hints on big-needle knitting. They are all great items to make for an upcoming event when you are in a hurry.

We hope you enjoy big-needle knitting projects and still have time for other joys in life.

The items in this book are made with big needles (sizes 10½ and larger) and worsted and bulky yarns. The combination of big needles and thicker yarns makes for a project that works up quickly. For some projects, thinner yarns can be worked double to create a bulky feel.

Don't be afraid to try the bigger needles even if you are not used to working with them. The stitches are formed the same as for any knitting project. The needles may feel a little clumsy and awkward at first, which may seem surprising if you have been knitting for a while, but as you continue knitting, the needles will soon feel comfortable in your hands and you will find the project you are working on is well on the way to completion.

Knitting Basics

We've included the basics needed throughout this book here for your reference.

Cast On

Leaving an end about an inch long for each stitch to be cast on, make a slip knot on the right needle.

Place the thumb and index finger of your left hand between the yarn ends with the long yarn end over your thumb and the strand from the skein over your index finger. Close your other fingers over the strands to hold them against your palm. Spread your thumb and index fingers apart and draw the yarn into a V, **Fig 1.**

Place the needle in front of the strand around your thumb and bring it underneath the strand on your index finger, **Fig 2.**

Draw through loop on thumb, **Fig 3.**

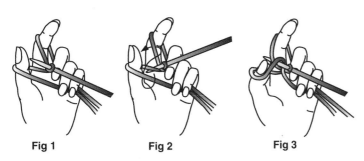

Fig 1   Fig 2   Fig 3

Drop the loop from your thumb and draw up the strand to form a stitch on the needle.

Repeat until you have cast on the number of stitches indicated in the pattern. Remember to count the beginning slip knot as a stitch.

Knit (k)

Insert tip of right needle from front to back in next stitch on left needle.

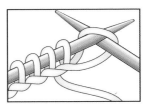

Bring yarn under and over the tip of the right needle.

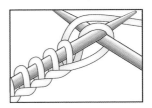

Pull yarn loop through the stitch with right needle point.

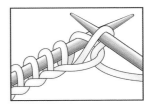

Slide the stitch off the left needle. The new stitch is on the right needle.

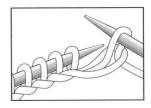

Purl (p)

With yarn in front, insert tip of right needle from back to front through next stitch on the left needle.

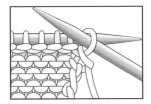

Bring yarn around the right needle counterclockwise.

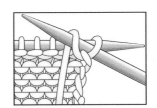

With right needle, draw yarn back through the stitch.

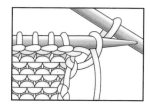

Slide the stitch off the left needle. The new stitch is on the right needle.

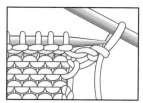

Increase (inc)

The most frequently used increase is to knit 2 stitches in 1 stitch. To use this increase, knit in the next stitch in the usual manner, but don't remove the stitch from the left needle. Place the right needle behind the left needle and knit again into the back of the same stitch. Slip original stitch off the left needle.

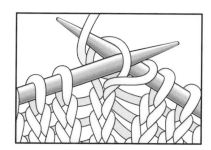

Another increase is a Make 1 (M1) or invisible increase. For this increase, insert the left needle from front to back under the horizontal loop between the last stitch worked and the next stitch on the left needle.

With right needle, knit into the back of this loop.

Decrease (dec)

Knit 2 together (k2tog)

Put tip of right needle through next 2 stitches on left needle as to knit. Knit these 2 stitches as 1.

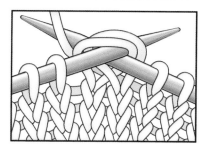

Purl 2 together (p2tog)

Put tip of right needle through next 2 stitches on left needle as to purl. Purl these 2 stitches as 1.

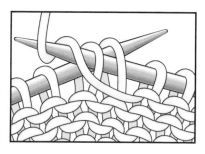

Slip, Slip, Knit (ssk)

Slip next 2 stitches, one at a time, as to knit from left needle to right needle.

Insert left needle in front of other stitches and work off needle together.

Bind Off

Knit first 2 stitches on left needle. Insert tip of left needle into first stitch worked on right needle and pull it over the second stitch and completely off the needle.

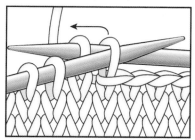

Knit the next stitch and repeat. When 1 stitch remains on right needle, cut the yarn and draw tail through last stitch to fasten off.

Stripe-It-Rich Turtleneck

Design by Scarlet Taylor

EASY

Sizes

Extra-small (Small, Medium, Large) *Instructions are given for smallest size, with larger sizes in parentheses. When only 1 number is given, it applies to all sizes.*

Finished Measurements

30½ (33½, 37, 40) inches

Materials

Bulky (chunky) weight yarn, 12 (18, 18, 24) oz, 215 (324, 324, 432) yds, 340 (510, 510, 680)g each plum (A), goldenrod (B), denim (C)

Note: *Photographed sweater was made with Lion Brand Wool-Ease Thick & Quick, plum #145, goldenrod #187 and denim #114.*

Size 11 (8mm) 16-inch circular knitting needle (for neck band)

Size 13 (9mm) knitting needles or size needed to obtain gauge

Tapestry needle

Stitch marker

Gauge

10 sts and 14 rows = 4 inches/10cm with larger needles in St st

To save time, take time to check gauge.

Special Abbreviations

SSK (Slip, Slip, Knit):

Sl next 2 sts knitwise one at a time, insert left needle through fronts of these sts; k2tog.

M1 (Make 1):

Inc 1 by inserting LH needle under horizontal strand between st just worked and next st, knit through back lp.

Pattern Stitches

Stockinette Stitch (St st)

Row 1 (RS): Knit.

Row 2: Purl.

Rep Rows 1 and 2 for pat.

Knit 2, Purl 2 Ribbing (k2, p2 ribbing)

Row 1 (RS): K2, *p2, k2; rep from * across.

Row 2: P2, *k2, p2; rep from * across.

Rep Rows 1 and 2 for pat.

Stripe Pattern

For Front and Back

*9 rows A.

9 rows B.

9 rows C.

Rep from * 2 times more.

Work rem rows in A.

For Sleeve

9 rows A.

9 rows C.

9 rows B.

9 rows C.

9 rows A.

9 rows B.

9 rows C.

Work rem rows in A.

Instructions

Note: *Stitch count includes a selvage st at each end of row for seam. These sts are not included in finished measurements.*

Back

Following Stripe pat for back, with larger needles and A, cast on 42 (46, 50, 54) sts.

Ribbing

Work k2, p2 ribbing for 9 rows, ending with a WS row.

Body

Row 1 (RS): With B, working in St st and Stripe pat, k1, SSK *(see Special Abbreviations)*, knit to last 3 sts, k2tog, k1. (40, 44, 48, 52 sts)

Row 2: Purl.

Work even in St st in Stripe pat as established until piece measures approx 10½ from beg, ending with a WS row.

Shape armholes

Row 1 (RS): Continuing in Stripe pat, bind off 2 sts, knit across.

Row 2: Bind off 2 sts, purl across. (36, 40, 44, 48 sts)

Row 3: K1, SSK, knit to last 3 sts, k2tog, k1. (34, 38, 42, 46 sts)

For Sizes Extra-small and Small only

Continue with For All Sizes.

For Sizes Medium and Large only

Row 4: Purl.

Row 5: K1, SSK, knit to last 3 sts, k2tog, k1. (40, 44 sts)

Continue with For All Sizes.

For All Sizes

Work even in Stripe pat as established until piece measures approx 18½ (18½, 18½, 19) inches from beg, ending with a WS row.

Shape Neck

Row 1 (RS): Working in Stripe pat, knit across first 10 (12, 13, 14) sts; join 2nd skein of yarn, bind off next 14 (14, 14, 16) sts; knit rem sts.

Note: Work both sides at same time with separate skeins of yarn.

Row 2: Purl to last 3 sts on first side p2tog, p1; on next side p1, p2tog, purl rem sts. (9, 11, 12, 13 sts on each side)

Shape Shoulders

Row 1 (RS): Bind off 3 (3, 4, 4) sts, knit across.

Row 2: Bind off 3 (3, 4, 4) sts, purl across.

Row 3: Bind off 3 (4, 4, 4) sts, knit across.

Row 4: Bind off 3 (4, 4, 4) sts, purl across.

Row 5: Bind off 3 (4, 4, 5) sts.

Bind off rem 3 (4, 4, 5) sts.

Front

Work same as back until piece measures approx 17½ (17½, 17½, 18) inches from beg, ending with a WS row.

Shape Neck

Row 1 (RS): K11 (13, 14, 15) sts; join second skein of yarn, bind off 12 (12, 12, 14) sts; knit across.

Note: Work both sides at same time with separate skeins of yarn.

Row 2: Purl.

Row 3: Knit to last 3 sts on first side, k2tog, k1; on next side, k1, SSK, knit across. (10, 12, 13, 14 sts on each side)

Rows 4 and 5: Rep Rows 2 and 3. (9, 11, 12, 13 sts on each side)

Work even, if necessary, until piece measures same as back to shoulders, ending with a WS row.

Shape Shoulders

Work same as for back.

Sleeves

Make 2

Ribbing

Working in Stripe pat for sleeve, with larger needles and A, cast on 26 sts.

Work in k2, p2 ribbing for 9 rows, ending with a WS row.

Body

Row 1 (RS): With C, working in St st and Stripe pat, k1, SSK, knit to last 3 sts, k2tog, k1. (24 sts)

Row 2: Purl.

Continue in Stripe pat, inc 1 st by M1 *(see Special Abbreviations)* each side [every other row] 0 (0, 0, 1) time(s), then [every 6th row] 10 times. (44, 44, 44, 46 sts)

Work even in Stripe pat until sleeve measures approx 20½ inches from beg, ending with a WS row.

Shape Cap

Row 1 (RS): Bind off 2 sts, knit across.

Row 2: Bind off 2 sts, purl across. (40, 40, 40, 42 sts)

Row 3: K1, SSK, knit to last 3 sts, k2tog, k1. (38, 38, 38, 40 sts)

For Sizes Extra-small and Small only

Continue with For All Sizes.

For Sizes Medium and Large only

Row 4: Purl.

Row 5: K1, SSK, knit to last 3 sts, k2tog, k1. (36, 38 sts)

Continue with For All Sizes.

For All Sizes

Bind off.

Assembly

Sew shoulder seams.

Neck Band

With RS facing, beg at right shoulder seam with circular needle and A, pick up and knit 40 sts evenly spaced around neck edge, place marker for beg of rnd. Work in rnds of k2, p2 ribbing for approx 3½ inches. Bind off loosely in rib.

Set in sleeves. Sew sleeve and side seams. Weave in ends.

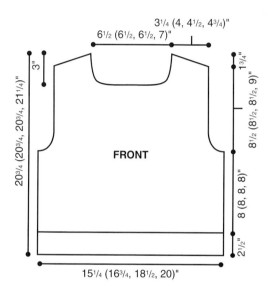

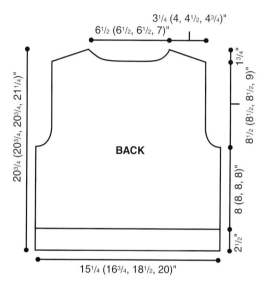

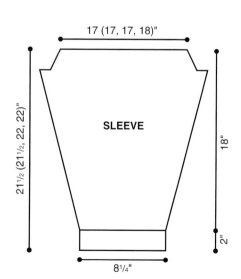

Warm & Toasty Trio

Design by Carolyn Pfeifer

EASY

Sizes

Scarf: 6 x 60 inches

Muff: 12-inch long x 15-inch circumference

Hat: 24-inch circumference

Materials

Medium (worsted) weight yarn, 17½ oz (975 yds, 500g) off-white (A), 3½ oz (195 yds, 100g) black (B)

Note: *Our photographed set was made with Bernat, Berella "4" natural #08940 and black #08994.*

Size 10½ (6.5mm) knitting needles or size needed to obtain gauge

Yarn needle

Gauge

14 sts and 24 rows = 4 inches/10cm

Special Abbreviation

K1B (Knit 1 Below):

Knit next st in row below needle, sl both sts off needle. (Fig 1)

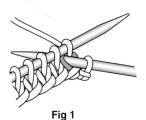

Fig 1

Pattern Stitches

Garter Stitch

Knit every row.

Rib Stitch (on even number of sts)

K1, *K1B *(see Special Abbreviation),* k1; rep from * across to last st, k1.

Instructions

Scarf

With B cast on 20 sts.

Rows 1–4: With B, work Garter Stitch pat.

Rows 5–18: With A, work Rib Stitch pat.

Rows 19–22: With A, work Garter Stitch pat.

Rows 23–32: With A, work Rib Stitch pat.

Rep Rows 1–32 nine times more.

Next 4 rows: With B, work Garter Stitch pat.

Bind off knitwise.

Finishing

Sew long edges of scarf tog.

Fringe

Cut 6-inch strands of B. Use 2 strands for each knot. Fold strands in half, insert crochet hook from back to front through stitch, pull fold through to back. Pull ends through fold, pull tightly. Make knot in each stitch across each short end of scarf.

Muff

Make 2

With B, cast on 44 sts.

Rows 1–4: With B, work Garter Stitch pat.

Rows 5–14: With A, work Rib Stitch pat.

Rows 15–18: With A, work Garter Stitch pat.

Rows 19–28: With A, work Rib Stitch pat.

Rep Rows 1–28 twice more.

Next 4 rows: With B, work Garter Stitch pat.

Bind off knitwise.

Finishing

Sew all sides tog. Fold piece in half and stitch sides tog to form a tube.

Hat

With B, cast on 66 sts.

Rows 1–4: With B, work Garter Stitch pat.

Rows 5–24: With A, work Rib Stitch pat.

Rows 25–28: With A, work Garter Stitch pat.

Rows 29–38: With A, work Rib Stitch pat.

Rows 39–42: With B, work Garter Stitch pat.

Rows 43–56: With A, work Rib Stitch pat.

Rows 57–60: With A, work Garter Stitch pat.

Rows 61–70: With A, work Rib Stitch pat.

Rows 71–74: With B, work Garter Stitch pat.

Row 75: With A, [K4, k2tog] 11 times. (55 sts)

Row 76: [K3, k2tog] 11 times. (44 sts)

Row 77: [K2, k2tog] 11 times. (33 sts)

Row 78: [K1, k2tog] 11 times. (22 sts)

Fasten off, leaving a 12-inch length for sewing.

Finishing

Thread end into needle and pull through rem sts. Pull thread tight. Sew ends tog. Fold up first 14 rows for cuff.

Blue Skies Baby Blankie

Design by Helen Stenborg

EASY

Size

Approx 30 x 46 inches

Materials

Medium (worsted) weight yarn, 12 oz/340g
 each off-white (A) and blue (B)

Note: *Our photographed afghan was made with Caron Simply Soft, soft blue #9712 and off-white #9702.*

Size 11 (8mm) 29-inch-long circular knitting needle or
 size needed to obtain gauge

Size K/10.5/6.5mm crochet hook (optional for edging)

Gauge

10 sts = 4 inches/10cm with 1 strand each of A and B held tog

To save time, take time to check gauge.

Pattern Stitches

Seed Stitch (even number of sts)

Row 1: *K1, p1; rep from * across.
Row 2: Knit the purl sts and purl the knit sts.
Rep Rows 1 and 2 for pat.

Open Work

Row 1: *K10, Seed Stitch pat across next 4 sts; rep from * across, ending k10.
Row 2: *P10, Seed Stitch pat across next 4 sts; rep from * across, ending with p10.
Row 3: *K1, [yo, p2tog] 4 times, k1, Seed Stitch pat across next 4 sts; rep from * across, ending with k1, [yo, p2tog] 4 times, k1.
Row 4: Rep Row 2.

Instructions

Note: *Afghan is worked in rows on circular needle with 1 strand of each of A and B held tog throughout.*

Lower Border

With 1 strand of A and B held tog, cast on 78 sts.

Work Seed Stitch pat for 6 rows.

Body

Row 1: Work Seed Stitch pat across first 6 sts, work Row 1 of Open Work pat to last 6 sts, work Seed Stitch pat across last 6 sts.

Row 2: Work Seed Stitch pat across first 6 sts, work Row 2 of Open Work pat to last 6 sts, work Seed Stitch pat across last 6 sts.

Row 3: Work Seed Stitch pat across first 6 sts, work Row 3 of Open Work pat to last 6 sts, work Seed Stitch pat across last 6 sts.

Row 4: Work Seed Stitch pat across first 6 sts, work Row 4 of Open Work pat to last 6 sts, work Seed Stitch pat across last 6 sts.

Rep Rows 1–4 until piece measures 46 inches.

Upper Border

Work 6 rows of Seed Stitch pat.

Bind off in pat.

Edging

Note: *If not familiar with a single crochet stitch, see instructions below.*

With crochet hook and single strand of B, sc around edge of blanket, working 3 sc in each corner; join with sl st in first sc. Fasten off.

Single Crochet (sc)

Begin by making a slip knot on the hook. To make a single crochet stitch, insert the hook in the edge of blanket. Bring the yarn over the hook from back to front. Draw the yarn through the blanket and onto the hook. Again bring the yarn over the hook from back to front and draw it through both loops on hook (Fig 1).

Fig 1

Stylish Bolero

Design by Svetlana Avrakh

EASY

Sizes

Extra-small (Small, Medium, Large, Extra-large) *Instructions are given for smallest size, with larger sizes in parentheses. When only 1 number is given, it applies to all sizes.*

Finished Measurements

To fit chest size: 34 (38, 42, 46, 50) inches

Materials

Bulky (chunky) weight yarn, 10 (10, 10, 15, 15) oz, 510 (510, 510, 765, 765) yds, 280 (280, 280, 420, 420)g each soft taupe (A) and misty shades (B)

5 BULKY

Note: *Photographed bolero was made with Bernat Soft Bouclé, soft taupe #22011 and misty shades #22927.*

Size 11 (8mm) straight and circular knitting needles or size needed to obtain gauge

3 long stitch holders

Stitch markers

Gauge

8 sts and 14 rows = 4 inches/10cm in pat

Pattern Stitch

Ridge Pattern

Row 1 (RS): Knit.

Rows 2–4: Purl.

Instructions

Back

With 1 strand each of A and B held tog, cast on 30 (32, 34, 36, 38) sts. Mark beg and end of row.

Row 1 (WS): Knit.

Rows 2 and 3: Knit.

Work Ridge pat 4 times. Mark beg and end of row. Place sts on holder. Cut yarn.

Left Sleeve

With 1 strand each of A and B held tog, cast on 16 (17, 17, 18, 18) sts.

Row 1 (WS): Knit.

Rows 2 and 3: Knit.

Work in Ridge pat, inc 1 st each end [every 9th row] once, then [every 10th (8th, 6th, 6th, 6th) row] 4 (5, 3, 3, 6) times. (26, 29, 25, 26, 32 sts) Inc each end [every 12th (10th, 8th, 8th, 8th) row] 1 (1, 4, 4, 2) times. (28, 31, 33, 34, 36 sts)

Continue even until piece measures approx 18 (18½, 19, 19½, 20) inches ending with a Row 4 of Ridge pat.

Fasten off.

Right Sleeve

Work as for left sleeve. Do not fasten off, slip rem sts onto a st holder.

Body

Beg with Row 1 of Ridge pat and circular needle work as follows:

Joining row (RS): Work in pat across 28 (31, 33, 34, 36) sts of right sleeve, continue in pat across 30 (32, 34, 36, 38) sts from back st holder, work in pat across 28 (31, 33, 34, 36) sts of left sleeve. (86, 94, 100, 104, 110 sts)

Work even in Ridge pat until piece measures 6 inches from joining row, ending with a Row 4.

Front shaping

Row 1 (RS): K1, k2tog, knit to last 3 sts, k2tog, k1. (84, 92, 98, 102, 108 sts)

Rows 2 and 3: Purl.

Row 4: P1, p2tog, purl to last 3 sts, p2tog, p1. (82, 90, 96, 100, 106 sts)

Continue in Ridge pat, dec 1 st each end of every other row 4 times.

Dec 1 st each end [every row] 5 times. (64, 72, 78, 82, 88 sts)

Bind off 4 sts beg next 2 rows. Place rem 56 (64, 70, 74, 80) sts on a stitch holder.

Neck Edge Border

With RS of work facing and circular needle, beg at right sleeve and joining row, pick up and knit 25 sts up right side of body to beg of shaping, pick up and knit 18 sts around right front shaping, work in Ridge pat across 56 (64, 70, 74, 80) sts from stitch holder, pick up and knit 18 sts around left front shaping, pick up and knit 25 sts down left side of body to joining row and left sleeve. (142, 150, 156, 160, 166 sts)

Place 3rd set of markers each at end of needle.

Note: *Rem of border is worked with WS becoming RS.*

eg with RS row, work 15 rows in Ridge pat, reversing
S to WS.

nit 2 rows.

ind off knitwise (WS of collar).

lace 4th set of markers.

inishing

ew side seams matching first set of markers with
rd set and 2nd set of markers with 4th set. Sew
eeve seams.

desired, use pin or broach to keep front closed.

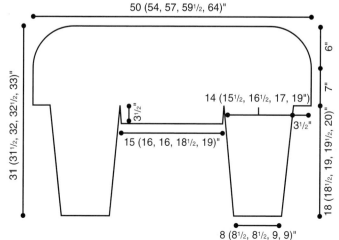

Chunky Cuffed Cap

Design by Patsy Leatherbury

EASY

Size

21-inch circumference

Materials

Bulky (chunky) weight yarn, 165 yds
(150g) plum (A), 55 yds (50g) blue (B)
Note: *Our photographed cap was made with
a bulky weight wool blend.*
Size 11 (8mm) knitting needles or size needed
to obtain gauge
Tapestry needle

Instructions

Body of Cap

With Color A, cast on 62 sts.

Row 1 (RS): K2, *p2, k2; rep from * across.

Row 2: P2, *k2, p2; rep from * across.

Rep Rows 1 and 2 until piece measures 5 inches, ending
with a WS row.

Shape crown

Row 1: [K2, p2tog] 15 times, k2. (47 sts)

Row 2: [P2, k1] 15 times, p2.

Row 3: [K2, p1] 15 times, k2.

Row 4: P2tog, [k1, p2tog] 15 times. (31 sts)

Row 5: [K1, p1] 15 times, k1.

Row 6: P1, [k1, p1] 15 times.

Row 7: [K2tog-tbl] 15 times, k1. (16 sts)

Row 8: Purl.

Row 9: Knit.

Row 10: [P2 tog] 8 times. (8 sts)

Cut yarn leaving a 6-inch tail. Thread tail through rem
sts and fasten off.

Cuff

With B, cast on 18 sts.

Rows 1 and 2: With B, knit.

Rows 3 and 4: With A, knit.

Rep Rows 1–4 until piece measures 19 inches ending
with a Row 2.

Bind off with B.

Finishing

Place RS of cuff to WS of body of cap, sew side edge of
cuff to cast-on edge of body of cap.

Sew back seam, sewing RS tog for body of cap, then
reversing seam to sew RS tog for cuff. Turn cap right
side out and roll cuff.

How to Check Gauge

A correct stitch gauge is very important. Please take the time
to work a stitch gauge swatch about 4 inches x 4 inches.
Measure the swatch. If the number of stitches and rows are
fewer than indicated under "Gauge" in the pattern, your
needle is too large. Try another swatch with a smaller size
needle. If the number of stitches and rows are more than
indicated under "Gauge" in the pattern, your needle is too
small. Try another swatch with a larger size needle.

Abbreviations & Symbols

approx .... approximately
beg .... begin(ning)
cn .... cable needle
dec .... decrease/decreases/decreasing
k.. knit
k2tog.................................... knit 2 stitches together
LH .... left hand
lp(s) .... loop(s)
M1 .... make one stitch
mm.. millimeter(s)
p.. purl
pat(s) .... pattern(s)
p2tog.................................... purl 2 stitches together
psso .... pass slipped stitch over
rem.. remain(ing)
rep.. repeat(ing)
rev St st .... reverse stockinette stitch
RH .... right hand
rnd(s) .... round(s)
RS..right side
sk.. skip
sl.. slip

sl 1k .... slip 1 knitwise
sl 1p .... slip 1 purlwise
sl st.. slip stitch(es)
SSK .... slip, slip, knit these 2 stitches together—a decrease
st(s) .... stitch(es)
St st .... stockinette stitch
tbl .... through back loop
tog .... together
WS .... wrong side
wyib..with yarn in back
wyif..with yarn in front
yo .... yarn over

* An asterisk is used to mark the beginning of a portion of instructions to be worked more than once; thus, "rep from * twice more" means after working the instructions once, repeat the instructions following the asterisk twice more (3 times in all).

[] Brackets are used to enclose instructions that should be worked the exact number of times specified immediately following the brackets, such as "[K2, P2] 3 times."

( ) Parentheses are used to provide additional information to clarify instructions.

Standard Yarn Weight System

Categories of yarn, gauge ranges, and recommended needle and hook sizes

Yarn Weight Symbol & Category Names	1 SUPER FINE	2 FINE	3 LIGHT	4 MEDIUM	5 BULKY	6 SUPER BULKY
Type of Yarns in Category	Sock, Fingering, Baby	Sport, Baby	DK, Light Worsted	Worsted, Afghan, Aran	Chunky, Craft, Rug	Bulky, Roving
Crochet Gauge Ranges in Single Crochet to 4 inch	21–32 sts	16–20 sts	12–17 sts	11–14 sts	8–11 sts	5–9 sts
Recommended Hook in Metric Size Range	2.25–3.5 mm	3.5–4.5 mm	4.5–5.5 mm	5.5–6.5 mm	6.5–9 mm	9 mm and larger
Recommended Hook U.S. Size Range	B1–E4	E4–7	7–I-9	I-9–K-10½	K-10½–M-13	M-13 and larger

The above reflect the most commonly used gauges and hook sizes for specific yarn categories.

Skill Levels

BEGINNER
Beginner projects for first-time knitter using basic stitches. Minimal shaping.

EASY
Easy projects using basic stitches, repetitive stitch patterns, simple color changes and simple shaping and finishing.

INTERMEDIATE
Intermediate projects with a variety of stitches, mid-level shaping and finishing.

EXPERIENCED
Experienced projects using advanced techniques and stitches, detailed shaping and refined finishing.

Metric Chart

INCHES INTO MILLIMETERS & CENTIMETERS (Rounded off slightly)

inches	mm	cm	inches	cm	inches	cm	inches	cm
1/8	3	0.3	5	12.5	21	53.5	38	96.5
1/4	6	0.6	5 1/2	14	22	56	39	99
3/8	10	1	6	15	23	58.5	40	101.5
1/2	13	1.3	7	18	24	61	41	104
5/8	15	1.5	8	20.5	25	63.5	42	106.5
3/4	20	2	9	23	26	66	43	109
7/8	22	2.2	10	25.5	27	68.5	44	112
1	25	2.5	11	28	28	71	45	114.5
1 1/4	32	3.2	12	30.5	29	73.5	46	117
1 1/2	38	3.8	13	33	30	76	47	119.5
1 3/4	45	4.5	14	35.5	31	79	48	122
2	50	5	15	38	32	81.5	49	124.5
2 1/2	65	6.5	16	40.5	33	84	50	127
3	75	7.5	17	43	34	86.5		
3 1/2	90	9	18	46	35	89		
4	100	10	19	48.5	36	91.5		
4 1/2	115	11.5	20	51	37	94		

KNITTING NEEDLES CONVERSION CHART

U.S.	0	1	2	3	4	5	6	7	8	9	10	10 1/2	11	13	15
Metric(mm)	2	2 1/4	2 3/4	3 1/4	3 1/2	3 3/4	4	4 1/2	5	5 1/2	6	6 1/2	8	9	10

American School of Needlework ®
excellence in instruction

DRG Publishing
306 East Parr Road
Berne, IN 46711

©2004 American School of Needlework
TOLL-FREE ORDER LINE or to request a free catalog (800) 582-6643
Customer Service (800) 282-6643, Fax (800) 882-6643

Visit AnniesAttic.com.

ISBN-10: 1-59012-108-2   ISBN-13: 978-1-59012-108-5   All rights reserved.   Printed in USA   5 6 7 8 9